A PRACTICAL GUIDE FOR MAKING YOUR FUTURE REAL

Create the Life You Only Imagined

LORRIE BORCHERT, M.A.

Introduction

If you have ever been to a nursing home and listened to some of the residents talking, chances are you have heard someone mention the life they "could have" or "should have" lived.

Many of the residents are filled with regret over choices they didn't make or choices that turned their lives into ordinary instead of into the life they had dreamed about.

They may have had dreams once, but life got in the way and they chose to put those dreams on hold. They resigned themselves to life as it unfolded in front of them.

In this book we will look at some of the commonsense reasons why people choose one life over another. Although these reasons may have been validated over the years, often there is still a glimmer of what life could have been "if" the choice had been different; if we had but been willing to go for it.

I, myself, had dreams of being a writer in my early 20's and ended up tucking that dream away to become a wife and mother to six. It wasn't until everybody was grown and left the nest that the writing dream began to surface again. I soothed it by becoming a prolific personal journal writer during the years I was an at-home mom and have reams of journals hidden in a trunk at my home.

Many years later I was asked to take on the position of national editor for a national monthly healthcare publication where I wrote technical healthcare-related articles each month, as well as the monthly editorial, but I always thought my real job was to get others to write articles of interest, so I didn't "really" consider myself a writer, and this part-time job didn't really fulfill the dream of being a published author with a book to my name.

Even though I've written this book I am still plagued with all the reasons why I'm not a real writer. The fact that I write makes me a writer and I need to own that. I was smart enough (finally) to get some coaching around this limiting belief (thank you Linda) and what I've learned is – no matter how scared and afraid I am – I need to lean into it – and just do it! So here it is!

How do you get in touch with those "woulda, shoulda, coulda" regrets and make the kind of choices that will let you move forward into finding your authentic life, tailored exactly as you always imagined it and free of regrets? I created this book to help those readers that are searching for answers, and want to get beyond the barriers to live the life they always imagined, but thought was impossible.

In Part I we will look at our life to date. We'll examine how we got here by the choices that we made. We'll delve into the limited beliefs that can keep us stuck and trapped and living a life that we had never imagined and create the regrets that we may be experiencing now or could experience at the end of our lives.

In Part II we'll look at four different concepts: do-overs, second chances, second journey's and how to envision and create the life you have only imagined up until now by creating a roadmap and action steps that will help you create and make your future real.

Journal exercises are available at the end of each chapter or you can purchase the Journal Companion separately and put all the responses to the exercises into that format. Either way, these exercises will prime the pump to get us thinking personally and in greater depth than we ever have before. You can choose your own journal at the store to record your notes as you read along and drill down to discover those lost and forgotten dreams that may have been sleeping. Choose one that has an interesting cover and appeals to your imagination.

I cannot stress enough how important it will be for your own self-discovery to complete these exercises. You will begin to see some movement and clues will be begin to emerge around that life that you imagine for yourself.

The writer Thomas Carlyle once said: "The best effect of any book is that it excites the reader to self-activity." My hope is that you will use this book in an interactive way so that the material presented really becomes part of your own search for those dormant dreams that once seemed so important.

If I can help you on the way to achieving your dreams – as your very own life coach – email me today for a free "Taste of Coaching." Don't forget to sign up for my free monthly newsletter below and follow my weekly Blog.

Lorrie

Email: lorrieborchertbooks@gmail.com
    Website: futuresmadereal.com

Part I

Living Big With No Regrets

Chapter 1

REGRET EXPOSED - A TIME FOR TRANSITION

A record number of people are retiring each day. In fact, according to Pew Research, 10,000 baby boomers are retiring daily and will continue to do so for the next 19 years! Imagine 10,000 people each day making the decision to retire and each one finding themselves in a unique valley of transformation.

In looking back at jobs they have held, children they've raised and relationships they've had with significant others and friends, they either have a sense of contentment and fulfillment or a sense of disappointment over some of the choices they made.

Many wonder what's next? Today age 65 is being called "the new 50," that time in our lives when we feel old enough to have mastered what life has thrown at us, but still feeling somewhat adventurous and wanting to make the next decade count for something.

Retirement is a transitional time zone that that provides an opportunity to choose what it is that we want to do next. Other transitional times include choosing a particular college or interviewing for a certain job, getting married or deciding to have a child. It is in that space, between now and then, that we decide to take on the next big thing. We can choose to live big without regrets at each of these important intersections in our lives.

This is a time to look both at the past and at the present to decide what might happen in the future. People of all ages wonder what will be the best route to this future life, but some seem to be drifting or feeling stuck in a rut or feeling powerless to change things, whereas others move confidently to the future they planned.

As we look back over our lives we want to believe that our efforts counted for something. No one wants to waste the precious life we have been given. We all want to live a life with meaning and to believe that our life made a difference.

"Shoulda, Woulda, Coulda" (A song title by Beverly Knight)

At age seven, what did you want to be when you grew up? How about at age 14 or at age 21? Can you remember the eagerness you felt when you realized that you had a choice? Can you remember the elation you felt when you decided that this was "it!" Or how you felt when you shared this discovery with others?

Did you experience approval and acceptance for your choice? Or did you receive disapproval that made you think that your choice seemed odd or wrong?

When you shared this discovery with others, did you experience a sense of approval for your choice?

Or were you told to get real and be more practical and responsible in your choice? In your life did you choose the more practical choice, or go for the one you'd been talking about ever since you were seven?

As we grow up and head to college we often have the experience of choosing what we want our life's work to be. Sometimes we choose our childhood choice as our college major but often times a new choice appears and at the time this seems to make more sense.

These choices seem to show up from out of nowhere but they may have come as a result of our reading or lectures or observing someone we admire. We may find a hidden talent or imagine ourselves in a particular role and so it makes total sense to us to pursue a new and different path. It could also be a series of events, or classes that are open or changed, or maybe a summer school class that was not part of the scheduled program. Any number of scenarios might have caused students to veer from one course of study to another.

We begin to doubt the passion and excitement of the seven or fourteen year old and replace it with what we consider as a more mature and responsible path to follow. We decide or discard the earlier dream as perhaps being a childish or unrealistic idea.

Advisers and adults can also have a profound effect on what our choice may be. Perhaps, for practical reasons, they advise taking certain courses that surprisingly open up our consciousness to new knowledge or experiences that beckon us onto another path.

Parents often steer their children/teens away from fields of study that they judge may not be lucrative in the years ahead Artistic children and students often get this pep talk about being more practical and sensible about the future. All of us have heard the message about becoming a starving artist. When the artist child hears this message and imagines himself/herself hungry and cold and wondering how she will pay the rent, they often cave and look for a more stable course of study that will give them the needed financial security over their lifetime.

Many of these artistic-students-turned adults that made these more sensible choices are the ones who have serious regrets about the decision they made to choose a safer path. They imagine the life they could have had "if" they had but followed their passion and dream. Instead, they put one foot in front of the other and perform the job they were trained for and many times wake up and drive to work despising the choice they made. The guilt they feel when they think this way makes it easier to push that earlier dream away and decide to just forget about it.

After college we enter the workforce and this becomes another transitional time zone where choice enters in. More often than not, however, this choice takes us farther away from our childhood dream or our college choice. It could be that we settle for what is offered, understanding that there are no available jobs in the area that we may have had our heart set on or the money, hours and working conditions are too good to pass up. So we jump on it and find out afterward that we feel as though we settled.

In today's economy, it is not unusual to jump from job to job. Maybe we are being offered more money or more responsibility or the opportunity to work from home or have flex hours.

Technology has worked its way into most jobs, so it has become an essential tool that everyone must know. But what if you didn't have the opportunity to learn those skills because they did not exist back then? In today's workforce it is expected that you will keep up with all of the emerging technology that businesses install to stay ahead of the competition.

Often time's college students leave college without being able to find work in their chosen field of study. They are forced to take a job that they have no interest in or aptitude for, just so they are able to pay their bills. And so the dream, once so exciting and filled with passion and determination gets buried, stuffed down and forgotten like an old quilt, buried in a chest up in the attic.

Is it any wonder then, after a lifetime of work, they retire and wonder "now what?" They judge they are too young to sit in a rocker all day but not sure what to do next.

For many, this is the time of life that brings us face to face with the sense of longing about what we might have become "if" we had only been willing to take a chance.

It's hard to say goodbye to old dreams. It is easier to roll them around in the "coulda, shoulda", category because when we do that there is still a slight glimmer of hope. Once we say goodbye and close the door on that dream, we no longer continue to long for it.

But, if you are in a place right now where there is an opportunity to do a quick review of your life and a chance to shift forward into another journey or another path, then take some time to revisit the real reasons that you are not on another path and understand that it may have been the best you could have done at the time.

Let's fast forward back to this very moment as you are reading these words. As yourself if you are feeling happy and fulfilled in the life you are currently living. Take a few moments to really examine it and don't worry if you end up saying "no, I'm not happy or I feel as though something is missing or I feel lost and I don't know what I want to do, that I have no idea!"

∽

JOURNAL EXERCISES:

Exercise 1   What did you want to be when you grew up?

Exercise 2 – What did others want you to be?

Exercise 3 – What messages did you get about your choice?

Exercise 4 – What did you study in school?

Exercise 5 – Would you make the same choice?

Exercise 6 – Whose fault is it? Who do you blame for where you are today?

Exercise 7 – See yourself in the role you might have chosen

Exercise 8 – Evaluate your past choices - would you make them differently if given the choice?

Chapter 2

THE ROAD NOT TAKEN

"Two roads diverged in a yellow wood, And sorry I could not travel both And be one traveler, long I stood And looked down one as far as I could To where it bent in the undergrowth; Then took the other, as just as fair, And having perhaps the better claim Because it was grassy and wanted wear, Though as for that the passing there Had worn them really about the same, And both that morning equally lay In leaves no step had trodden black. Oh, I marked the first for another day! Yet knowing how way leads on to way I doubted if I should ever come back. I shall be telling this with a sigh Somewhere ages and ages hence: Two roads diverged in a wood, and I, I took the one less traveled by, And that has made all the difference.*

Robert Frost

WHAT PATH DID YOU CHOOSE?

I have always loved this poem, especially the part about the fact that he took the less traveled road. I've have wondered what there is about this sentence that evokes this feeling within me.

Then I think, maybe it is because I wish it had been me who had the courage to make that kind of choice. I think back and realize that in my own life I moved along with the rest of the crowd, deciding that my desire to be a writer was just that, a vague desire but totally unrealistic. I let my inner critic fill my head with stories that seemed plausible at the time, and in listening to them, they kept me safe from stepping out onto that road less traveled.

In using the road as our metaphor, we can easily see that it serves to offer us choices and paths, crossroads and intersections.

INTERSECTIONS

These are places where we can stop, breathe, recalibrate, reconsider and then move on. Most roads have turns where we're forced to choose whether to veer off one way or the other when we come to a fork in the road.

There are times we may make a choice that, in hindsight we decide may have been the wrong choice. Perhaps we thought, as we were paused at the intersection, that this upcoming turn would mesh with who we were at that moment or would take us to the place where we might find ourselves. However, now we have come to understand that we have some regret that we did not take the turn that would have brought us elsewhere sooner.

Life is a journey, a day-to-day living out of the decisions we have made - good or bad, right or wrong - based on what we knew at the time. As we age we gain insight and wisdom and we can often see that another choice may have made for a different outcome, maybe even a different life.

IS THERE STILL HOPE?

Regardless of how old we are when we begin to look backward at the expanse of our whole life, we still wonder why we made some choices and not others.

Perhaps you can remember hearing or reading about authors that were about an ordinary mother and who carved out a little time each day maybe between the laundry and the toddler's afternoon nap to write their novel. We all know J.K. Rowling who wrote her now famous Harry Potter books in a coffee shop on a white legal pad, while sipping cups of coffee.

We are all given the same 24/7 amount of time during the week, however some choose to carve out little chunks of time to pursue something that speaks to them from a passion point of view. Others may choose to use that time to take a walk or read a book or watch a movie or take a nap. Some authors tell how they arise before everyone else in the house to find their time to write before the household wakes up and needs them.

For me, it makes me question just how strong my desire was to be a writer. I told myself, surely if I really wanted to pursue a career as a writer then couldn't I have found time in spite of the fact that I had six kids and a traveling husband? I felt lucky in those days to find time to write a few paragraphs in my daily journal.

WHAT COULD STILL BE POSSIBLE?

Many people say to themselves, "I wonder what it would have been like, if only I..." and they try to imagine what life might have been like if they had only chosen differently. Watch for an exercise that asks you to do just that, later in the book.

They find themselves daydreaming about what it might be like if they could capture some of it right now in their current life and, for a moment or two, the concept seems almost doable, but then it fades away and they realize that this is the life they chose. What good is it to wish we were living another life, and we tell ourselves, to just get on with this one.

We are always so ready to shut the door and slam it against what we let go rather than look for a way to pick it up, turn it over and examine it to see if it could still be possible and still be incorporated and blended into our current life.

Haven't you met people who tell you that they always wanted to be a writer, painter, world traveler, etc., but for whatever reason they never pursued that path? As they grew older that thought is still nudging them and they think perhaps that time has passed them by... but is this true?

What we want to create is called " a start," it's a way to see what might still be possible – and no, it not too late to start but it could be if we let it go.

Although it's not too late to start, we must decide to act on the nudges and inklings that are coming from deep within.

In Martha Beck's book, "Finding Your Own North Star", she explains that the "essential self" is that part of our personality and being that we are born with and is the deep essence of who we are. As we grow up, we often have the other side of our personality, the "social self", take a greater role because it's purpose is to engage socially and it is very quick to make sure that we don't do something that will embarrass us.

Over time we lose touch with the essential self that is key to guiding us to the place we call our right life. It's the part of us that lights up and feels so right when we touch on a thing or discover a passion. Martha explains in her book that getting in touch with our essential self helps us to find the path that will lead us to our north star (to ourselves).

Even so, we often disregard our essential self because we judge the social self to be more in alignment with what is right and proper and what society expects from us. Some people find the social peer pressure so uncomfortable that they stay in roles that they have outgrown years ago. It's just too hard (they think) to make the change they wish they could make.

Suffice to say that we probably haven't been listening to our essential self for a long while. Hopefully this book will help you get in touch with what lights you up – what makes you feel alive – and what makes you say, "ah ha!!"

Remember, some of the greatest adventures of our lives are often the result of taking a risk and deciding to turn a corner just to see what might happen.

∼

JOURNAL EXERCISES:

Exercise 9 – Draw out the roadmap since you were age twenty

Exercise 10 – What is hindsight telling you?

Exercise 11 – What were the boundaries that stopped you?

Exercise 12 – What do you catch yourself wishing and dreaming about?

Exercise 13 – What do you worry about? What do you think others would say? Does this stop you?

Exercise 14 – How do you cope when you come to an intersection?

Chapter 3

UNCOVERING FORGOTTEN DREAMS

Many times we set aside our dreams as impractical and nonsensical . We tell ourselves we were just kids back then and did not have the same responsibilities we have today. We go on to think that we don't have time in our busy schedule to worry about a dream that we gave up on years ago. Does this sound familiar?

Let's take a minute and decide that we can give ourselves permission to look for it. Let's browse, as you might in a crowded store or library for clues from the past that might give an indication of what used to bring excitement and a smile. We can begin our search in our childhood.

Who's Stopping You?

For many of us we have a ready explanation so that when someone causally asks us the question, "why didn't you become a writer?" – we have our answer ready. (In the coaching world, we call this "our story.")

Sometimes, it is another person who we put the blame on – "my teacher told me I'm a terrible writer" or on someone else's opinion – "well, after reading your writing, I'd advise not leave your day job" or a parent who may say something hurtful like "you'll never amount to anything!"

We shove down and repress any notion that, if given another chance, they might have been wrong. Naturally the parent or other adult/child who made the comment has long forgotten saying the hurtful phrase that we continue to keep alive within ourselves.

We attach personal meaning to the comments we heard and to the dream. We immediately feel judged as lacking and believe that the commenter must have been right. We begin to think that maybe the dream was too ambitious for us anyway, so we stop right then - in the fourth grade - and throughout our whole life.

What's Your Story?

Messages can come from anywhere. Maybe no one said anything out loud but maybe you compared yourself with someone else, like an author who already had a book published. We think internally that we'll never be that good or able to have the words to write at that level. It becomes all or nothing kind of thinking.

When we get right down to it, would you believe that it is probably "you" who is stopping you?

We forget when we have to start anything new that we are all beginners – not experts. So often times we are feeling our way along and we judge ourselves, and our attempts, as feeble because we forget that every successful person was once a beginner.

Many people have a deep belief within that they are not good enough and struggle with low self-esteem. This, they believe, is what is holding them back from living out their dreams. They use this as an excuse not to try something that they judge may be too far outside of their comfort zone. In many cases it may really be a fear of failure that holds them back from trying.

There are many books and stories about people who tried and failed many times and then finally succeeded. We often find stories like this with inventors who were trying to make things that had never been imagined before.

Think of poor Thomas Edison, Google tells us, "Thomas Edison's teachers said he was too stupid to learn anything! He was fired from his first two jobs for being non-productive. As an inventor, Edison made 1,000 unsuccessful attempts at inventing the light bulb."

The message here is, don't be afraid to start. Find a small way to go forward and try something out, whatever it may be. Spend some time researching and reading about it. Speak with others who have already mastered it. How long did it take them to get where they are now in their field?

In many cases we stop ourselves from trying to go for the gusto because of self-limiting beliefs and messages that we picked up along the way from random snatches of conversation that we've pieced together. We behave as though we were detectives at work on a complex murder scene. In the end, even though the puzzle is still incomplete, we buy into the story and carry it with us. Sometimes this story is still with us until we take our last breath. We have embraced the story so firmly there is no room for change.

When we think of the lost dream or the road we haven't taken, there is sometimes the associated limiting belief that, "I would never have been good at it anyway, so I'm glad I never bothered." This is one way we can shrug off the lost dream and make it seem as though it wasn't really all that important anyway!

∼

THE INNER CRITIC

Even though we are all grown up, we may still feel we have some inner authority within giving us messages. Do you encounter this problem? This authority may also be called the "inner critic." This inner critic can be helpful when we come up with a hair brained scheme or decide to do something dangerous. Then it's a good thing and very helpful. Its job here is to keep us safe and sound. (Oh, and not to appear too crazy to others!)

Personally I have lived with a very strict inner critic in my head! Nellie is always telling me what I can or can't do – trying (I think) to protect me and keep me safe, but she is really annoying and hard to live with! I've tried for years to quiet her down, and have even tried to kill her off, but she's very resilient and she doesn't respond to any of my attempts to tame her.

For instance, in my fledgling attempts to become a writer, Nellie has always said very harsh things to me. I think she tells me these things so that I will stay safe and be content to play small. For example, if I only write privately in my journal then the words are safe and I can't get hurt. Perhaps she also thinks that if I stay with the journal, then what real troubles can I get into out in the world?

One successful way that I have found around this critic is to continue writing after my morning journal pages are finished – and seamlessly I transition to other writing such as my blog, or my book or blog or newsletter. I think the inner critic is napping because she thinks I'm still doing the "safe" writing in the journal. She doesn't realize that I'm getting ready to thrust my writing out to prime time!

SELF TALK'S PURPOSE

Self-talk can be very negative and discouraging when it is related to lost dream. When negative self-talk is coupled with the critic, its goal will be to stop you from believing that you could actually go forth and resurrect that old dusty dream into a possibility.

Developing positive self-talk is one way to allow space so those dreams begin to feel safe and can peek out. For those who are more comfortable with the negative self-talk because this is what they have heard for years, they may need some outside motivation and stimulation to shift the internal message. Sometimes finding a positive quote that reflects what you wish to achieve can help, especially if you put it in a place where you will see it often during the day.

As I sit writing at my desk, I can see reminders, two white containers that are etched with the words

Write and Work Hard

Or the greeting card, pinned up on bulletin board that states:

Live with intention, walk to the edge, listen hard, practice wellness, play with abandon, laugh, choose with no regret, continue to learn, appreciate your friends, do what you love, live as if this is all there is.
(Mary Anne Radmacher)

I especially love the small wooden square that sits on the ledge above my desk with these words

No Regrets Only Lessons Learned

Find some inspiration and motivation to spur you ahead to your future life.

Henry Ford said,

"If you think you can, you can. If you think you can't, you can't."

How true this is!

It really is all about what we allow ourselves to believe is possible. This is why Olympians can accomplish unbelievable feats because they stay focused on the task ahead of them and keep positive self-talk as a way to encourage and push them forward instead of a way to keep them frozen and unproductive. They also visualize the end result – they see themselves actually accomplishing the goal and holding the gold medal.

We can learn to use these same tools to push us toward the goal we wish to achieve. We can learn to shut down the negative self-talk too and make a concerted effort to practice positive self-talk to ourselves.

JOURNAL EXERCISES:

Exercise 15 – What forgotten dreams did you put aside?

Exercise 16 – Do you find yourself waking up wanting to wake up those sleeping dreams? Say more.

Exercise 17 – My story is (fill in the blank with the story you tell yourself and others)

Exercise 18 – Pretend you are going to make a start. How would you go about it?

Exercise 19 – How have you been stopping yourself? How? Give examples.

Exercise 20 – What is your inner critic telling you? Listen and write down the things you hear. Which ones hold you back?

Exercise 21 – List 3 things you could do to address your own critic

Exercise 22 – What are your have to's and should's?

Exercise 23 – What positive self-talk do you use?

Chapter 4

RECOGNIZING THE RIGHT PATH

Think about the path you are walking along on today. Did you make a conscious personal decision to go down this path or did it just appear out of nowhere? Or do you wonder how on earth you got here?

Sometimes we choose our path with great deliberation – but sometimes we marry someone other than we thought...have a baby when we least expected one... or find ourselves in a job that has nothing to do with what we studied for or had a passion for.

Examples might be:

- Getting married to the one I love
- Choosing a college
- Deciding on a career field
- Having a child
- Losing a Job
- Other:

Life has a way of shaking things up, especially when we create elaborate plans for our future. Have you heard the one about "We make plans and God laughs."

Circumstances change, the economy changes, we change and the path we once started down have many twists, turns and intersections. It's not always as clear as it once was when we were young and everything looked so bright and shiny.

FINDING NEW ROADS

Maybe you have been walking on a path that you really wish was something different – maybe the path over there looks greener and seems easier to travel. You wonder to yourself, "How can I get off this treadmill? Telling yourself, "I'm going nowhere fast and I hate it!" You can hear family and friends making comments about "What a bad economy we're in"...so you just put one foot in front of the other, put your head down, and tell yourself you can endure it. This is how we get stuck staying on the same path – the one that we have outgrown and isn't serving us now. The path that some people stay on until the day they retire or the day they unexpectedly die early.

Have you ever had a synchronistic experience happen and suddenly, without warning, you find yourself on an entirely different path without a map?

WHAT IS OUR PARTICULAR PATH?

Each of us is on a path, what we need to understand about our path is:

- Is it where I want to be?
- Is my path serving me now or have I outgrown it?

- Is my current path in line with my values?
- Am I bored, stuck or on a dead end path?
- What other path/s appeal to me?
- What would I need to do to get there?

Sometimes we stand with one foot on each path. We may need to stay that way until we can decide which one works. We strategize to find ways to step over to fully embrace the new path. Sometimes we can integrate and merge two paths into one.... and sometimes, we can find the answer to the right path for our life – right now – right where we are.

Having a Choice

How many people do you know who continue to stay stuck and trapped due to a fear of letting go of the old in order to embrace the new? They may not express it out loud to others in terms of fear, but as they look at all of the areas in their lives that could be affected, it can feel overwhelming to move forward to complete the changes that may be required.

Staying stuck and feeling trapped is a state that many people find themselves living in. In fact, many have the sincere belief that there is no alternative for them and that the best thing they can do is to just stick with the situation until – the end (retirement or job lay off). This sense of feeling trapped as they dress and prepare for work each morning fills them with a sense of dread and distaste for this choice that they may have made years ago. They see no way out, no way to escape, so they tolerate the pain of it to have the security and benefits the job offers.

Although we all have the ability to make choices and to take action, it is precisely this combination of choice and action that creates the change in our lives. We may dream about different choices and even create an ideal world inside our head but it isn't until we combine a different option with a series of action steps that the change we only dreamed can happen.

This requires, however, a temporary disruption that can be both uncomfortable and stressful. Releasing stuck and trapped feelings adds a fresh new perspective to everyday living. Sometimes a change in responsibilities or a job transfer can offer the same benefits. Part-time jobs or volunteer opportunities can offer the same benefit as well.

Retirement planning is a good example of a time in our lives when choice appears. Retirees have an expectation that after all their hard work in raising a family and putting in a lifetime of hours into their jobs, that they can finally choose what they'll do in their spare time.

Some choose to take on adventure and travel. Some choose to move to a retirement-friendly environment. Some choose to stay closer to home and do volunteer work, putter in the garden and relax. Still others choose to work in a part time job or start their own business or write a book. This is a time when it's fun to have choices, as there is a lessening of outside pressure and a stage where they can finally let the unconscious desires bubble up.

It is also a time to move forward, to forge new experiences, meet new people and let this new life lead us to a path we may not have seen earlier in our lives. It can also be a time to look at those unexamined and sleeping dreams and a time to try them on and see which ones still fit after all this time.

We have within us the power to choose. So what will it be? Marcia Perkins-Reed in her book, Thriving in Transition reminds us, "If we fail to consciously visualize what we want to create our new situation will just perpetuate the mistake of the past. Unless we challenge ourselves through imagining how our lives could be better, we will tend to make choices that fall within the parameters to which we are accustomed."

~

ENGAGING IMAGINATION

We all have the ability to imagine. Some of us can even envision all the terrible things that might happen. Others have a vivid imagination complete with bells and whistles.

When we are trying to choose a path for our future, it's often useful to use our imagination to create a visual picture of just what we want it to be. When we link the lost and sleeping dreams of the past with imagination to envision the future we begin to see what our life could become.

In an earlier chapter we discussed the fact that we may have made previous choices based on the circumstances or responsibilities that were present at the time. We may have thought that this decision would provide needed money and security for our family, or it could have been the circumstance that this was the only job offered or available at the time. Whatever the reason we agreed to take the job and probably did not think much more about it at the time.

Searching for Clues

We can use these clues to help discover any hidden passions. In connecting the dots, have you noticed any unusual circumstances lately that you might describe as coincidences or synchronicity? This synchronicity could occur through meeting someone who could serve as a connector to your next path. Or it could happen by reading something or attending an event or in talking to someone you know who knows someone in the area of your interest. Some people refer to this kind of synchronicity as a "God wink."

Clues are all around us, we need only to recognize them. Stay aware and watchful for events and people who can serve as your personal connector and for clues to the path. Don't be afraid to try something different. Sometimes new experiences open the door to the dream you had years ago.

If you were looking at what else interests or engages you, then what does the vision board say about that? What did you already know and what surprised you? Keep your vision board where you can see it and it will continue to give you messages about different paths to follow – different dreams that may have been dormant.

Photos of anything that speaks to us are often used to build a vision board. . It could be the color of an object or the curve of a building or the hammock slung between two trees with the image of the ocean in the background. As we begin to glue these images and messages down to our board, connecting them in layers or next to each other, clues emerge. Clues that feel more or less like we'd like our future to look like.

TOOLS FOR DECIDING

As we are led toward a new path we are usually still standing on our old one. Sometimes we straddle two paths simultaneously or we step over and sample the newer path just to test it out to see if it would work better. We have been taught to think about making choices by using our heads and logic. Rarely do we choose based on how it makes our body feel. We ignore these cues, because they are too soft and such an "iffy" way to make an important decision. Yet we acknowledge that in our current circumstances there may be stress-related issues associated with our bodies. We also acknowledge that we may experience fear and tightness when we even think about the choice.

Learning to feel a "yes" within our body is an excellent way to understand that a choice we are considering making may be a good one to follow.

Most of the time we make our decisions primarily based on logic and we pride ourselves on choosing the one that seems to puts us in the most favorable light in terms of our responsibilities. I'm sure you have chosen this way in the past, we all have.

Some people use the Ben Franklin method. In this exercise we list all the pros in one column and all the cons in another and then agree to make the final decision based on the column that has the greatest number of entries. This takes out all the emotion and biases out of the decision strictly on pro/con criteria.

Others use friends and family to guide them to a choice, although later they may state that they followed the advice at the time, but ended up feeling very unfulfilled because they didn't really choose it for themselves.

JOURNAL EXERCISES:

Exercise 24 – Identify your own personal path - try to draw it out on paper or create a vision board.

Exercise 25 – What can you see that is true about your path? Do you see any patterns that you can recognize?

Exercise 26 – What makes you feel trapped?

Exercise 27 – What choices would you make today that are different than those you made previously? Why?

Exercise 28 – How good is your imagination?

Exercise 29 – Look for clues in your life that indicate what your future could look like

Chapter 5

LESSONS OF EMPOWERMENT

As we learned in previous chapters, we are responsible for choosing our life's path and there are plenty of intersections and forks in the road that give us new opportunities to choose again.

In reviewing some of the methods others use when faced with making choices and understanding how imagination can play a big role in plugging in options, we stand at the tipping point for deciding how we want our own future to unfold.

Likewise we can also choose to decide to live a regret-free lifestyle. When we make the decision to do so we often notice a change in our attitude and perception. If we shift our perception by fast-forwarding to a time in the future when we are older and see ourselves in conversation, we can try to eavesdrop and listen to our older self, sounding regretful about the things that we left undone. The dreams that we left hidden often produce a profound sense of regret that hangs in the air.

However, at this point it is too late to make amends or changes? Or must we must settle for whatever we choose, or not.

As you listen to this imaginary conversation you make up your mind that you'll do better in the days ahead and that you would allow some of the hidden dreams to surface. You believe that maybe you still have time – time to live it up – try it out – see what works. And this is when the most profound shift in attitude begins to unfold.

Suddenly we are no longer content with the ordinary "Same old/same old" daily life and we want to add in some pizzazz and try out new things, and live out our lives with gusto. And intention. That image of the much older version of ourselves stays with us. We see that we have a walker parked next to our rocker and we notice that our room is small and has an air of a hospital about it. Thinking about now, we long to have time to try our wings with new things before we reach this later stage in our life.

Suddenly we understand that it is in our control to choose and move forward on that decision, right now, while we do have time. We can empower ourselves and cross over the bridge that takes us from here to there. It's our choice to do it.

Victim Be Gone

Have you ever experienced feeling like a victim when asked the questions, "why didn't you ever pursue your dream to be a: _____ (fill in the blank).

Why didn't you?

In answering the question we may have added in or embellished reasons why we went in a totally different direction. We saw ourselves in the role of the victim because we blame others or the circumstances from preventing us from making the choice we wish we could have made.

Sometimes the reason we give paints us in an unflattering light and casts the blame elsewhere. Regardless of how our situation played out there was a role that we played that led to the outcome.

We need to understand how we let dreams and passions slip through our fingers. We need to own the role we played in the situation and, if possible, take the blame and forgive ourselves for the decisions we made.

I have found that once I learned to empower myself, the victim disappeared. In consciously choosing not to be a victim by choosing authenticity as a strong and present value in my daily life, I have begun to own who I am.

Choosing Authenticity

But I am For many years I wrote as though I was in hiding as I was afraid to display my writing in public. I was fearful of how it would be viewed. As I grew in my role as a writer, I have gradually opened myself up to sharing my writing with others.

I need to be real.... I need to share with others the truth of who I am and what I am about. Now when I write a blog entry, for instance, and the authentic me is exposed, sometimes I still want to run and duck for cover but I am more comfortable in letting it go and having people see and understand the real me.

TELLING the World and Others

As you work toward this value called authenticity, how are you feeling now about sharing it with others?

When we understand that the only thing we know to be absolutely true is the fact that "everything is changing," we know that this is also true about ourselves.

As I grew and learned and changed throughout my life I have tried to be brave and step out of the shadows and let others see and know the real me through my writing. There were times that I felt fearful and afraid and thought I perhaps they wouldn't like what I wrote or me. The lesson I learned was an important one, keep going... no matter what!

You may know people who act in a certain way and they are fully aware of it and say they do not care what others think. They may feel so secure in themselves that it becomes the other person's responsibility to "deal" with it.

Today social media and online blogging are very popular and perhaps you have put yourself "out there" into cyberspace. It is a different feeling than writing the same material in a personal journal. Now that it is out there, you are out there, and you have a moment or two to reflect on whether this is the "authentic you" that was sent forward.

Much of blogging and Face Book postings are about being able to "find your voice" – the tone, the interest. When we live in balance we are aware of what is important and the concept of living in a regret-free environment seems easy and doable.

Today I stand by my own writing. I am not looking to blame others or circumstances if I fail. I own it and fix it and move on. My approval comes from within – not from others who may or may not like what I am about. It can take time to find that voice both in your speaking and in your writing voice.

Journal Exercises:

Exercise 30 – What would an imaginary conversation from then future sound like? Write it down.

Exercise 31 – My victim story (fill in the story that you tell yourself and others).

Exercise 32 – Examine your own authenticity - are you living it yet?

Exercise 33 – Name a situation/s where you feel/felt out of balance.

Exercise 34 – Examine the concept of balance and alignment in your life - do you feel grounded and in balance with who you really are? If not, why not?

Exercise 35 – Examining your own voice on social media. Is it your true voice? Is this the authentic you? If not, who is it?

Chapter 6

WHAT CAN YOU SAY FOR SURE?

Many people live out their lives with no though of regret, but once they get older, they begin to look back with what some call "20/20 hindsight" and replay certain decisions that they made earlier in their lives.

We gain perspective as we move about in our daily lives but it is often a piece here and there. When we get to the place in time where we review our life in its entirety, we can begin to connect the dots and gain a greater perspective, a larger picture, of our whole life.

PERSONAL LEGACY

Perhaps you can remember a favorite grandmother reminiscing about her life. Unconsciously she is creating meaning for her life. By reviewing the length and breadth of her life to date she connects events and people in order to share the meaning of her life with others. This is a purposeful, reflective and retrospective process that dwells on the past in order to come to peace with the past and the present.

We all have a basic need to review our past as we move forward into our future. Psychological theorist Erik Erikson named the developmental stage for people aged 65 and older as "Ego Integrity vs. Despair." He stated that in this period, people look back to determine whether they have led happy, successful lives. If they feel that they've been successful and productive then they develop feelings of contentment and integrity, but if they see their lives as being unsuccessful, they may feel depression and despair instead.

When we review the span of our lives to date, we stand in a transformational space. A space where we can make the decision to make changes in ourselves that will change the course of the path we are on or learn to be content with where we are and in what our life represents. It is at this point that we see all the crossroads, forks and intersections that presented us choices along the way. We can clearly see that in some cases we turned left instead of right and that path led to a spouse and children and at another crossroad we chose to turn right and found a new career choice we'd never even considered before. One can use this key time to review the gaps and choices and identify why we may have chosen differently.

This review is important because as you begin to dig deeper into the "whys" of the choices that you made you begin to see more clearly and in some cases feel the regret that the choice created. These are often feelings and thoughts that were stuffed away and we chose not to deal with at the time. Let's take them out and dust them off and get to the bottom of them, to own the choice by taking responsibility and decide not to blame others.

In Part 2 of this book, we will learn to put them aside and step into creating the life that you may have only imagined.

The good news is that we don't necessarily need to wait until we are 65+ years old to take time to review our life and make decisions on changes that we'd like to see. Once we have done the examination and have a full understanding of the choices we made at the time and why, we can put those to bed and move on into crafting choices that do not contain regret.

~

JOURNAL EXERCISES:

Exercise 36 – Let's try to perform a brief life review. Find out what you identify as regrets.

Exercise 37 – Identify any gaps in choices you may have made

Part II

Do-Overs, Second Chances and Second Journey's

Chapter 7

DO-OVERS

I n Part 1 we have spent time understanding how you got to where you are in your life right now. As we move into Part 2 we'll draw a line in the sand and travel forward into imagining and creating the life we have always wanted to live.

If we look through the lens of wanting to have no regrets in our life, then we can learn to think big and decide to choose a different path for our future. We have choices and one of them is choosing to try something else. Perhaps something that feels closer to what our heart's desire is.

In this next section we will look at concepts such as do-overs, second chances and second journeys. Exercises are provided to give you a chance to brainstorm and dream. So many people have no idea of who they want to be when they grow up (and these are older adults). No plan equals staying right where you are.

We sum up this transformational journey back to where we started, with the concept of choosing to live a regret-free life doing what we only imagined our life could be. At the end of the day we don't want to be sitting in the rocker talking about our regrets.

How We Think **About Do-Overs**

Personally, I dislike having to do things over and over. It's a negative reaction and I immediately begin to think about how I have messed something up and now I need to start all over again to fix it.

I also dislike having to back up to go forward. This is a pet peeve of mine and I notice that it happens when I leave my sunglasses home and I must decide if I can still go on without them or if I must go all the way back home. Most of the time I make the choice to go forward instead of turning around and going back.

I am not sure when this belief first made its presence known but I do know I have been believing it for a long time.

It plays out for me in other ways too - such as when I write my blog. I just want to post it as I wrote it. I don't want to go back to the start and begin again with the whole editing process; and if it requires a second or third review, it sets my teeth on edge and I want to pull my hair out.

So how can someone entrenched with a belief this strong decide to write a book about do-overs?

Well, recently I've been thinking about the concept of do-over in a new light. I am now seeing it in terms of taking a few steps back and then deciding what I'd rather do instead.

I find that in shifting the thinking around, my do-over gets a slightly different result. I invite you to try it too.

Where Do I Find Do-Overs?

Do overs can be lurking in many different places in our daily lives. What about your morning routine?

We all have areas that we would like to change. Some of these behaviors are engrained like ruts in a dirt road. We have always done things this way and it has just become second nature.

Are there changes you wish you could make yourself do? Things like:

- Create a walking routine before breakfast?
- Get up earlier so you are not late again?
- Eat a healthy breakfast?
- Write 3 pages before showering?

Maybe when we try out that early morning walk we then decide it just too hard to get up every day and make it happen, so we take the easy way out and we just roll over and hit the snooze button. This results in our being late again and having no time for a healthy breakfast.

Some people slip in a walk at lunchtime or after work. They may have tried the morning routine and realized the timing was not the best so they continued the do-over a few more times at different times of the day to find what would work for best.

Another big area of do-over seems to be around diet and food and our health. Because we live in a society where it is easy to eat whatever we want, when our Doctor tells we that we need to eat differently for our health we may understand it, but we aren't happy about making the shift in our thinking or in deciding how to execute this kind of a do-over. It is often too easy to exit into the drive through window because we're hungry and feeling deprived.

Do-Over Research

Sometimes we must research what needs to change in our lives so that we know how far we need to back up before we can go forward into the new belief. This helps in both the planning and execution of the steps it will require creating the shift.

DOING Over a Career

Let's look at another area where people are most anxious to perform a do-over and that is switching over to another job or career.

Many people get up each morning when the alarm sounds to head off to a job that no longer serves them. They dream and wish and imagine that they could make a significant change but feel trapped and with reluctance settles into the realization that this is what it is. For some, this is a matter of practicality or responsibility.

Is it wrong to dream and imagine doing something that could bring us joy and contentment? Are we doomed to stay put when we judge it is not a good fit?

A do-over of this magnitude requires a strong big picture vision of what the desired outcome would look like. A big picture view paints the future with a broad brush and it can feel like the perfect rendition of what the perfect career or job would be.

It doesn't have to be perfect or complete. Sometimes we are just given a small piece of what the vision is and we may have to wait awhile for another piece to appear. It can be like an unfinished puzzle - unclear until all the pieces come together to form the picture.

Unless one has an idea or a vision for what would be ideal, most people stay stuck right where they are. They cannot quite see what the whole vision is. They cannot imagine all the steps and hard work that will be involved to make it a reality. These are all valid points to consider. Many people are working in one job while learning about the dream job in their off hours.

Sometimes it is possible to do more than dream. Maybe a course or two becomes available that will give additional knowledge in the area you are headed. Other times a part-time or volunteer position becomes available where hands-on experience can be gained.

Perhaps they aren't really committed at this time to take a big leap, but they may be open to taking a smaller step in their current job situation. They can scan the current environment to look for opportunities that are more in line with the vision they have uncovered for the future.

DIGGING DEEPER

Questions we might ask:

- Do we have the education and knowledge to do that kind of a job today?
- Or would we need to gain more schooling, knowledge or experience?
- Would we know how to get that?
- Could we afford it?
- Would our family support a decision like this?
- Could we do it simultaneously while working in our current job?
- Are we committed to doing the time consuming research required?
- How long would it take?

SHIFTING the Outcome

When we create a shift in our strongly held belief system, we begin to see something we thought we thoroughly disliked in a whole new light.

If we make the effort to step back, it gives us the time to plan differently and to launch the plan with a new expectation of what the outcome could be.

~

WHERE THE SHIFT OCCURS Is In Our Thinking

In my case, the going backward before going forward belief, I can shift to wanting to check that I have everything I need before leaving the house. It may seem like a subtle shift, but it will prevent me from having to come back for lost items and I can confidently move ahead, knowing I have everything I need.

~

REFRAMING The Limited Belief

Reframing the belief can help us to take in, accept and try out a new belief. Sometimes we need to tweak it a few times in order for us to really buy into it and have it feel better than our original belief.

Seeing it in a positive versus negative light also helps our unconscious mind to take it in and adopt it. Most of us will not adopt a new belief that doesn't feel right. We may not be able to articulate the exact reason why it doesn't feel right, we just know it isn't. This happens when it isn't locked in place. We can then readjust it until it fits. A good example might be when we are fitted for glasses and the technician makes adjustments until it fits just right and we can see clearly.

Let's ask some questions to dig a little deeper:

- What if some of your beliefs were off and no longer represented the truth?

- What if some of the items in our belief system just weren't true?
- What if we picked them up from a TV show or a conversation we had with someone who had a different set of beliefs?

Let's try an example: What if, when you were six years old you connected something you overheard with something you thought it meant and you created a belief about it that you have held onto ever since. Has this ever happened to you?

But what if, when you connected the dots of meaning at age six that you didn't assign the correct meaning and so your belief has really been "off" all these years? Over the years you made it be your truth when perhaps it never really happened the way you thought it did.

It could be that your limited beliefs are the reason you have never quite gotten the results you hoped you would get.

So why not line them up and see if you can apply some do-over thinking to put you back in alignment with a belief system that is true to who you are today?

Do you remember hearing the phrase, "Change your thoughts and you'll change the result?" You may have wondered exactly what they could have meant.

All of us have developed our belief system over time. What we believe to be true about ourselves, loved ones and basically about what we hold dear. These are all part of our belief system. These also include messages we received from parents, friends, spouses, the TV, Internet and church.

SHIFTING Into A New Belief

Let's say that we watched the documentary called "Forks over

Knives" about the health benefits of eating a plant-based diet. We loved the concept and it sounded like just what we needed to shift our eating patterns so that we'll lose weight and also improve our overall health, but here's the thing:

How do we get started?

- Do we have to throw out all the food in our fridge and pantry?
- What do we buy instead?
- What kind of recipes do we use?
- Will we like a plant-based diet?
- Can we convince the family to come along with our decision?

It's understandable that making such a large change can be filled with doubt and confusion. Doing a little research will help us to create a plan for what to purchase, what recipes to use, and what to stock in the pantry/fridge.

Decision:

We must decide whether or not to adopt a new pattern, idea or plan. We might be saying to ourselves,

- Can we live with this change?
- Will it get me to where I want to go? (Weight loss, better health)?
- Will I really buy in or revert to my old ways?

Preparation:

If the answer is 'yes", then we move into the preparation time. Here we get all that we need in order to adapt to this new plan/idea:

- Make a list of all the items we will need
- Make a trip to the store and stock up
- Eat up or give away the non-plant items in our fridge/freezer so we won't be tempted

Create and Schedule a Start:

Then a do-over such as this requires a date on which we will officially launch the new eating plan:

- Mark the calendar when we will start the new plan
- Tell at least one other person so we make ourselves accountable.

Implementation:

- Create the first week's menu's
- Begin by showing up and starting
- Begin to understand that a big change like this takes time to adapt. Both in terms of research, preparation and action steps. Beyond that it takes time to adapt to the new belief system. We may not take to it right away, or we may decide to do some of it, but not all of it.
- Be kind to yourself during this transition time. It's easy to slip backward for a variety of reasons. Learn from the "why" you reverted back and in your do-over learn to carry proper snacks in the car so that you will not be tempted again.

Lastly, Assess Your Progress:

- After one week and again after two weeks assess your progress.
- Note any weight changes on the calendar.
- Celebrate!

We have all heard that it takes 21 days to adopt a new behavior, so give yourself time. In this case we would have gone shopping three times in that 21-day period. We would have tried 21 new recipes and we may be seeing that the scale has reflected weight loss or our clothes are fitting more loosely.

We might also begin to notice that we are feeling differently due to our new eating plan.

Review Your Progress:

After one month assess all of the benefits of this plan for our health. Now we have the choice of deciding whether to adopt this new eating plan for our life.... or just for now.

MISTAKES AND FAILURES

Sometimes things don't always go the way we imagined or planned. We find ourselves wishing we could have another chance to make it right. Maybe we wish for a do-over where we can incorporate hindsight (which they say is 20/20) into the new plan for success. Often the second time around works out perfectly fine and we wish we had gained these insights the first time.

What Changed?

In many cases it could be attributed to our attitude. Perhaps we shifted our focus or became aware of a step that we had neglected to take as we prepared for the do-over.

Do-over's are part of our every day life but we may not call our actions by that term.

Sometimes we just let the mistake or failure stand, either because we cannot fix it or we give up and just decided to leave it be.

Research has shown that our body will keep that negative emotion stored and it will reveal itself as anger or failure turned inward at some point in the future.

Journal Exercises:

Exercise 38 – What are some things you don't want to have regrets about?

Exercise 39 – What is an example of a recent do- over in your life?

Exercise 40 – Can you identify any shifts in your thinking that have taken place over time? Or recently? List them.

Exercise 41 – Find examples do-overs in your morning routine. Do you see any patterns? List them.

Exercise 42 – What routine would you like a do-over on?

Exercise 43 – What does success look like to you? Write it down. Remember - this one is about success for you.

Exercise 44 – What lights you up? Makes you shine?:

Exercise 45 – What have you learned from failure? List the lessons.

Exercise 46 – Examine some limiting beliefs that may no longer be true for you. List them

Chapter 8

SECOND CHANCES

S ometimes we all wish we could just be given a second chance in our lives. Maybe it's career related or maybe we wish we had made a different choice about something or wish we'd done more research or had more courage or been braver about the choices we made.

But often times we just feel stuck with our choice and believe there is no way out. We believe we just have to stick with it until - the end - or till we retire, get fired or find something better.

But what if a second chance suddenly presented itself?

- Would you recognize it as such?
- Would you use it to make a profound change?
- Could you use it as a catalyst to make a different choice and propel yourself out of the current rut you are in?

Some may ask, what is the difference between a second chance and a do-over? By way of explanation, a do-over refers more to a project or task, whereas a second chance has more substance to it. Sometimes, on the golf course, we may hear someone wish they could have another chance to hit the ball to get a better lie. When the golfer takes the shot again, it's called a mulligan and it counts toward the scoring.

When we think of the concept of a second chance, it is often used in reference to another opportunity, such as a new career, job, mate or marriage.

A second chance presumes that we have taken the first chance and then something has happened during the execution of this choice that creates a desire to be given a second chance. Perhaps we made a mistake and wish we could be given another chance to fix it or to choose again. There may also be a change either within us or perhaps with our job, such as downsizing or retirement that offers another chance. A break up, divorce or death can often create an opening for a second chance.

An example of a second chance that we can all relate to is the lottery winner. Now, with the addition of this sum of money, the winner is automatically given a second chance to choose:

- To keep or ditch the current job
- To take a risk and create a new career
- Or quit or retire from an unfulfilling job
- Or have the freedom to check out other options that may not have been financially possible in the past

A second chance is like getting the "get out of jail" free card in Monopoly. It suddenly gives us options that we never had available before.

A second chance usually has something else involved that serves as the catapult that sends us automatically into a new and different situation. It is unexpected and we do not always seek it out for ourselves, however it can propel us into a life we could only have only imagined but never thought possible.

A do-over is usually accomplished by us - making a decision and then re-doing an action..

Often we hear of people who have had a brush with a serious medical condition and who were either cured or healed speak in terms of having been given a second chance at life. They embrace the second chance and step out of their ordinary comfort zone and feel like they have been given a new lease on life. They vow they will make changes in their life so they will not end up like this again (if possible).

We do not need to wait for an illness or a tragedy to strike us to change our current circumstances. We can choose to have a second chance any time we need it.

Today many of us have a GPS tracking system in our cars and on our phones. When we put in our destination it takes us there. When we craft a second chance action plan, we must do the same thing. Maybe you remember the quote that states, "A goal without an action plan is just a wish." In this book we want to dream but we also want to be practical so that we can make our dreams come true.

What Would You Do If You Were Given a Second Chance?

If someone asked you if you wanted a second chance to live the life you always imagined, how would you respond?

Most people would pause to think because they would not have a ready answer. A few might respond with the vague idea of retirement and a few more may add in some travel to an exotic and far off land, but again, nothing specific.

The lack of a ready answer occurs because we are so busy trying to live our lives every day that we don't have time to think about changing to accommodate a different kind of life.

Typically, because we haven't thought it through we might mumble a negative reply such as:

- How much would it cost?
- How much time would it take?
- How much change would be required?
- Would I be able to make the leap and still pay my bills?
- How would it affect my family?

Once these are all added up, it remains easier and more cost-effective to stay right where we are, so we do.

Excuses We Tell Ourselves:

- I'm too old
- I don't have time
- I don't have money
- I put those dreams away a long time ago
- Its painful to go over what I really wanted to do, but settled for something different
- What would other people think of me if I were to make these changes in my life right now?
- I have no idea what I'd do!

We let these negative and limiting beliefs keep us stuck and grounded right where we are, but what if all these thoughts and beliefs were banished and did not exist?

DO NOT let any negative voice tell you that you can't do what you are dreaming. Just tell the voice, thank you, and Let's see what you can come up with!

Dreams are possible. The only real limitation that holds you back is your thinking. It's not time, money, talent, ability or availability. No, it's the fact that you haven't yet let yourself imagine it without any barriers.

CRAFTING a Second Chance

Close your eyes and see it - open your body compass to feel it - let yourself, just for a moment, see yourself in this new environment. Check out your face. Are you happy? Do you have a sense that this is it?

Grab your journal and pen and write down, as fast as you can, any and all of the details you saw when you allowed yourself the permission to go where you wanted to be.

Write until you capture it and then elaborate on anything else that would make this picture complete, such as, what did it smell like or how did it feel, hot or cold? Any other details could be helpful.

CREATING An Action Plan

It's great to see all the great possibilities that can come from an exercise like the one above. We all know its fun to dream, but it takes steady action to take yourself from where you stand today to where you want to be tomorrow. It doesn't just happen, it is a crafted plan that is done in advance that lays out all the steps and in some cases, identifies the roadblocks and obstacles that might be in the way.

So let's go with what you came up with in the last exercise, the one that really lit you up, and look to see if you can create a path from your current location to that imagined life. Let's call this our roadmap. This little visual will help you map out your current location and your future location. It allows for several milestones along the way.

Milestones represent the big things that have to change as we move along the path, things like:

- Changing jobs or retiring;
- Selling the house
- Changing locations, etc.
- Differences in income

Each of us will have our own milestones to overcome on our second chance journey.

Let's not forget that some of the biggest obstacles on the this part of the journey are related to our thinking and our ability to sabotage our dreams by believing and engaging in the negative self talk that is created by our inner critic.

Instead, try to suspend those beliefs, because most of the time they aren't true. Continue with a new mantra of "I can and I will, just watch me!" It is possible and you will prevail if you don't bog yourself down. Try to suspend other people's beliefs also. They may not like or want you to dream beyond where there is some kind of control or reliability that is somehow threatened by your wanting more.

Remember we are crafting our own individual second chance. When we use our own imagination, creativity and authenticity to create it, then it becomes our own. When we invite suggestions from others about how we should craft it, then we lose that sense of our own creation. Not that there shouldn't be communication with others but the place for it is after the creativity portion has been created and a penciled destination has been arrived at. It is so easy to become discouraged and derailed due to how others perceive we should be living our life.

We often do this to ourselves as well when we let the inner critic have control over us and we believe all its negative warnings.

Research tells us that ninety percent (or more) of what the critic tells us is false. Don't be afraid to dream, imagine and believe that a second chance destination is possible and can be yours. Having a plan and sticking to it will guarantee success.

Second Chance Lotto

Let's imagine for a moment that you have been given a second chance. In fact, here's a second chance ticket with your name on it.

It seems incredible that you have been lucky enough to have been given this ticket...this second chance.

After all the excitement is over, your job is to decide what you will do with this gift.

Here are some ideas:

- What have you secretly wished you could do if you only had the chance?
- Would this unexpected opportunity create an opening to try something new?
- Could having a second chance help to change your life?
- Or change the projection of your career?
- Or change how you feel about yourself?

Again, let yourself imagine without boundaries, without the inner critic shooting each and every idea down. Let's continue:

- What do you wish for?
- What could change that is important to you?
- What would feel personally significant?

ENVISIONING the Future Using a Second Chance Approach

Research has shown that the clearer the image of our future appears in our brain, the more likelihood there is that our future will evolve into just what we had envisioned.

When we clear the path, we and make a way for the future to come to us.

Remember, the future will come whether we have planned it or not. We can be fearful of the outcome because we made no plan, or we can craft our future by imagining what we want and then working toward it by taking positive and calculated action steps.

How do you get from here to there? By taking a series small and deliberate action steps.

How do you know where you are going? We cannot reach the goal without knowing where it is and a map for getting there. As we stated before, it is up to us to create the roadmap. No one else can do it for us.

Second chances often occur while we are still in the midst of our first chance. Because it is while we are here that we begin to imagine something different for ourselves, to acknowledge that this chance doesn't fit or feel right and that a second chance must be made.

Let's imagine a creek where you have the first chance on one side and the second chance on the other. You cannot reach the other side until you let go of the first and create a plan for crossing over.

Our own life is like that as well. First we envision the picture of what it looks like and make it as clear as we can, then we decide what steps are needed to get there.

Journal Exercises:

Exercise 47 – You just won the lottery, now what?

Exercise 48 – What would you imagine that would change in your everyday life? What would you do with the money? How would you take your future into consideration?

Exercise 49 – Give yourself permission to dream.

Exercise 50 – Try your hand at creating a blueprint for your second chance journey

Exercise 51 – Creating your own second chance. How would you go about doing it?

Exercise 52 – Envision your future - write down what your perfect day would look like in your future.

Chapter 9

SECOND JOURNEYS DEFINED

Perhaps the easiest way to understand a second journey is in making the conscious decision to choose another path from the one currently being traveled. It is different from a second chance because it is usually on a larger scale and often permanent. It follows along a different path.

Some examples might include:

- A separation or divorce
- A new job in a totally different subject
- A move to a different town, state or country
- Going back to school for a different subject
- Retiring with options open

Typically we give some thought to the fact that we are being drawn to something different and we will need to make some changes. Our road map may not yet be fully fleshed out and the future lying at the end of the path is not quite clear - yet we are the active participant in choosing it.

Even though we know all this, we find ourselves drawn to the concept of this second journey...and we know, instinctively, that we will be changing and are okay with taking that on to get to the new life we are imagining.

- Even though we are scared
- Even though we haven't fully worked it out
- Even though we know it will be very different
- Even though we know it will mean significant change in our life

RETIREMENT AS A SECOND JOURNEY

Retirement can offer a great set of circumstances that will propel us onto a second journey whether we are ready or not!

For many people, this is the only second journey they will ever take. They will live their present life and then suddenly it is over, as they know it. What follows is either planned or not, but either way the routine that made up their every day life has probably changed. For some this feels like a death and they go through a period of mourning. It can feel like they are being pushed out of their comfort zone and into an area of life that they are not familiar with. The balance has tipped in favor of free time without deadlines or projects and it can feel very disorienting. For others, they can't wait to release the job that may have felt as though they were shackled and had no way to get free. They see being free at last as an awesome state to be in - but now what? That seems to be the question for so many folks ready to embark on the next chapter of their lives.

THE GAME PLAN

In May, 2016 the Motley Fool wrote "The expectation is that 10,000 boomers will exit the workforce each day between now and the end of the next decade. Some additional financial facts provided by Motley Fool include that 59% of boomers will rely heavily on Social Security; 45% of boomers have no retirement savings; 30% of boomers have postponed their retirement plans; 30% of boomers stopped contributing to their retirement accounts, and 44% are lugging around debt. Add to this the fact that seniors are living longer than ever with the average 60 year old living for another 21 years."

Perhaps you can personally relate to the statistics stated above and you believe that your own retirement will need to put off or forgotten as you work to get yourself on an even keel. Even if all of these statistics apply in your case you can still envision a future that incorporates some of the dreams you have carried with you all these years. Of course it takes some inner exploration to uncover what you wish the future to be and then create a plan to get there.

Here are a few examples:

Wish you could travel but have only a little money in the budget?

- Read travel books from the library
- Watch travel shows and then follow-up with books on selected areas.
- Try out different foods from a particular area or culture.
- Become an expert about a place you wish you could visit but do not have the funds to visit in person.
- Soak in the culture through music and art that can be found online and for free in the library.

A plan for retirement is often mapped out by a financial planner or by the Human Resources Department at the job, but there is often no additional help in mapping out what the rest of your future will look like. There are no action steps to follow and no real goal established.

It is no wonder than so many new retirees feel bewildered and off-kilter until they find their way. Unless the retiree has done some dreaming and planning about what an ideal future looks like to them, they continue to remain stuck in place.

Have your seen the marketing phrase used by a financial planning TV ad that asks the question, "Are you in the zone?" What they are referring to is the five-year period before the planned retirement. This, according to the TV ad, is the time that they advise for planning, adjusting and tweaking retirement monies to be set-aside for the retirement years.

Where is the zone planning to help the upcoming retiree create the roadmap and action steps so that when the time arrives they will be ready? This is where a life coach with experience in helping couples and individuals plan for their ideal futures can be a big help. The life coach will help the individual/couple to imagine and dream about the future that will inspire passion and an "aha" realization because it will spark a deeply held desire.

No time or money for your own life coach? Then try working through the exercises in this book and it's journal companion to make your own customized plan. It doesn't matter how you do it, what matters is that you have a plan and a dream for the future.

Visualizing The Next Chapter

It has been said that unless you know where you are going you can easily get lost and end up in a place you didn't count on.

It becomes crucial to visualize where the end point is. This point has been made before and it is important to stress it again because creating a big picture view with tweaks is what is needed until it looks and feels right. This always comes before taking the every day steps of the journey. Asking the question, "Will this step, this action bring me closer to what I have imagined my life will be?" In this way the journey has an outcome and when it is reached it will be apparent.

Envisioning the next chapter, while remaining knee deep in the current chapter, allows us to dream and plan about where we want to journey before we take any steps. For some it will remain only a dream-like state because there is no real understanding of how one would leap from here to there. (Really there is no one big leap, it is a series of small steps in both our mindset and our actions to cross from one chapter to the next).

We all know folks who have been thrust out into a new chapter without any preparation at all. A job could be lost, a spouse leaves or dies, a circumstance arrives that we could not have imagined and it must be incorporated into our present chapter or we learn to create something new out of what we have been dealt.

Some people view the concept of retirement as a new chapter, a second journey, a chance to begin anew, or to create a lifestyle that feels right. It may be that we dream and imagine what this new life-style can look and feel like and we may have done some advanced planning and have taken action steps to get there. We may easily transition into this new easy-go-lucky lifestyle or we may struggle because it doesn't quite live up to what we imagined it would be like. Maybe we have made the physical leap but may not have made the mental leap. We may be looking back over our shoulder to the way life used to be - to the lifestyle that we knew and felt comfortable with.

This concept of change has us in an uncomfortable and strange place. We aren't quite sure if it will work. We've all heard stories of folks who sold their homes and moved in early retirement and then moved back because the change was too great and they couldn't live outside of their comfort zone.

It takes a concerted effort to jointly paint the picture of what the necessary steps look like on the journey. This is a good way to look at it. When we take a trip we can't know before we start what we may see or the adventures that we might have. We may have a vague, broad idea but most of the time it changes when we actually take the trip. As we embark on this retirement adventure we must understand that it is a fluid journey and that things may change along the way and we need to be open to that happening.

After a bit, when the change we feared turns into our new comfort zone we find we are surprised that we were fearful at the start. Many say it turned out better than they thought and they are tweaking their new lives to suit them as they age, finding they now have more free time to pursue their individual and couple interests and learn to spend their days in leisure, travel or volunteering at a local charity.

What Needs to Change?

It all begins with our thoughts. So often we hear this statement. It is absolutely true that our thoughts are what give meaning to the items, people and situations in our life. For example, I have a blue and white canister on my counter that I use to represent my Dutch heritage as well as a reminder of the trip to Holland where I bought it. I have given it the honor of storing my loose tea inside and each time I use it, I am reminded of the meaning I bestowed on this canister.

As we pause to see what items we will choose to take on our second journey, we look to see what we have given meaning to. These are the items that we are most likely to choose to take along with us. Also, if we are moving to another location or dwelling we may look at our belongings and see which ones might fit the style or location and then give each a new meaning based on the role they will play in the second journey.

Our mindset is the biggest challenge standing between our desire to move forward and the fear that keeps us rooted firmly right where we are.

There is a tipping point that propels us forward or pulls us backward. Sometimes this is an outside source or circumstance that determines the direction. Sometimes it is the inner critic that is trying to protect us from change and the fear that comes from the imagined pain that the change will evoke. We are imagining that this pain may be more than we can tolerate and so our mind believes that this will happen and our second journey gets shut down as an idea that is not possible for us to pursue.

It is possible to change those negative inner messages into positive possibilities by learning to challenge the thoughts. Asking the simple question "why" to uncover the deeper worry and fear can help us understand why the critic is trying so hard to protect us and with some digging we can often come to an "aha" of understanding.

Is it possible to be scared to death and full of fear and make the change anyway? Of course it is. Think about the many thousands of people ho have boarded ships, leaving their countries behind to fearfully make the journey to a new country where they had no idea of what it would be like. It would have been easier in many respects to stay behind where their established lives made them feel comfortable, but in many cases circumstances forced the change.

When you think about your own second journey, what do you think you will need to take with you? This exercise is asking for practical and concrete thinking about what will change if you choose to follow the dream. Go along with it (as though you were all set to start off on your journey) and create the list. You may be surprised what you find that you'll be taking!

It is in being open to new things and new people and in expanding our thinking that we have gathered the important stuff for the journey.

The ability to move forward in a conscious state of awareness is crucial to stepping into the second journey. There is no benefit in being in a new place and constantly wishing to be back in the old place and having things exactly as they were. That might comfort and give familiarity, but it is important to continue to move forward and to create a new present with a mix of ideas and items from the past, as well as new ideas and enthusiasm for what this new future can hold. Packing a new attitude is crucial for the ability to experience the new journey from a non-judgmental perspective.

Understanding that change is hard for everyone, we need, nevertheless, to step forward into a space on this journey where it is all new and uncertain. "Didn't we want and need a change," we ask ourselves when we begin to worry and fear is biting at our heels? If that is true, then it is okay to acknow-ledge that it can be hard and different. It is an adjustment and the older we are when we make the adjustment the more ingrained we are with our daily pattern of living.

Wasn't the issue, "same old, same old" and we wanted something new and different? Well here it is. Now we have to learn to deal with whatever the new situation and environment calls for. Different is good - right?

An important ingredient for a successful journey is the awareness that life, as we know it, will change and that we could use some faith and belief that even though we have only a vague vision of the outcome we want, we will continue to head in that direction based on faith in ourselves. Curiosity and a sense of openness are also extremely helpful in moving forward. There will be new and unexpected situations that arise that we did not plan on and yet are part of the journey.

So pack up your attitude and let's get started!

ACTION STEPS **For the Second Journey**

We know you can't just step from here to there without some

kind of a plan and within that plan lies the series of steps that are necessary to complete before we can reach our goal. Let's start our second journey by beginning with the end result, which is our vision, and then work backward to see what needs to be accomplished before we can leave one place or situation for another.

By creating the "big picture" we can look at the whole project and begin to attach dates when we want things to happen:

- If we are moving, when will the actual move take place?
- If there is a job or career change, when will you leave one job and start another?
- If there is additional training or schooling involved, when will you go?
- If it is retirement time, what is the date?
- How much does it cost?
- When will you start?

Your decision to start on a second journey could begin several years before you physically begin the journey. Once the big picture is clear, then the process of organizing smaller action steps becomes easier because there is an understanding that unless these steps are taken, we cannot get to the next milestone in our big picture.

This is where a number of people fall down and give up long before they step out to take their second journey. Either they do not understand the concept or they are not willing to put in the work to get ready for taking the journey.

Any project manager knows that there are many milestones and action steps in any project they manage. The trick they use is to start with the end point in mind and then to work backward. In this way a calendar develops with all the major steps along the way mapped out.

Using this roadmap concept, anyone can visually see the milestones. They are the tasks that are cemented in place and often cannot be changed.

Examples Include:

- The lease is up on your rental on this date, so the date you move is (fill in the blank)
- This is the date I can take my social security and this is the date I set up for my in person interview (fill in the blank)
- This is the date that is most financially advantageous for me to retire (fill in the blank)
- This is the date I lost my job and I'm searching for the next opportunity

Dates that are anchored like the ones described offer a date that allows for actions to be scheduled on either side of the date. Examples might be, what must be finished and how long will it take and what actions need to be taken?

STARTING With The End in Sight

Let's look at a simple exercise below that examines where stand today, as well as, looks ahead to where we want to be. There are milestones that we will need to face along the way.

This is a simple way to get these down on paper so we can begin to see the big picture. It also allows us to see the smaller steps that need to be taken before and after the milestone is met.

Let's say you are going to sell your house. Getting it de-cluttered and ready to list are all action steps needed before the first milestone of listing the house. This part could have many steps that include giving things away, listing them on Craig's List, having one or more garage sales, finding an agent, deciding exactly when to list the house, staging it or emptying it depending on your particular situation. All this must be done before the listing happens.

So once the house is listed then there are additional steps such as, packing boxes, deciding if you will move by yourself or rent a company and making sure you have only the belongings you will need for your next living arrangement. Having the house clean and tidy for open houses and showings can take time and effort.

Perhaps the closing of the house is the next milestone. Once we close on the house we set the date for the actual move; lining up people to help or getting things ready for the moving company; getting services such as electric or cable disconnected in one place and connected in the new place.

Finally the day comes for the actual move. The truck is loaded and we say goodbye to the old abode and head toward the new.

Once we arrive there are tons of boxes and bins that must all be unpacked and new homes found for everything in the new space. We must set up bank accounts, turn on water, electric, cable, etc.

Once it has all been put away and we take a deep breath we realize we have reached our goal of getting from there to here. It didn't happen magically, there were many action steps and milestones along the way.

Try out this exercise for yourself for a goal that you would like to achieve. It could be a goal such as weight loss or adding more exercise into your life. Action steps indicate *how* you will achieve the goal. Remember that small, incremental turtle steps are often more helpful than trying to race through things. You do remember who won the race between the turtle and the hare!

∽

How To Manage The Shift

We have all heard the quote "Change your thinking, change your life" and truly this act of changing our thinking toward another way, an alternative path is often the first step in shifting into a second or even third journey.

When the goal is crystal clear we are somehow drawn to this outcome and by following our roadmap and moving through the actions steps we will achieve our goal, at least physically. But we need to also prepare mentally and emotionally so we can let go of the past and present by imagining what our future can be. Just think of a train track and use the metaphor of straddling this train train. This is a good way to think about how our mind is torn between two concepts, the present and the future.

There are many who give sage advice about how to stay grounded in the present while working toward creating the future. For a variety of reasons perhaps it is not yet the right time to make the physical shift but inside we can be busy imagining and planning for that second journey so we'll be ready when the time is right!

Journal Exercises:

Exercise 53 – Visualize your own game plan - write down how you would go about it.

Exercise 54 – What does the next chapter look like? Write it out.

Exercise 55 – Stuff for the journey - what would you take along? Leave behind?

Exercise 56 – What does my attitude shift look like? Can you feel it? What's different?

Exercise 57 – Starting with the end in sight - can you work backward to get to your future? Create a grid.

Chapter 10

CHOOSING TO LIVE A REGRET FREE LIFE

W e began this book with the concept of living a regret free life after we met the friends at the nursing home while in their rockers. We have explored what it could feel like to choose another chance or have another journey that might suit us better and leave us feeling contented and at peace that we lived our lives without regrets.

THE REGRET FREE ZONE

There is a sense of regret in all the things that they wished they had done but did not because of a myriad of reasons. Most, upon closer inspection, consisted of stories that they had been telling themselves about why they could not do a certain thing that they desired or to start on a career of their own choosing or live an authentic lifestyle as they wished. This story was a cover, an excuse for why they could not live the life of their dreams. So they often settled for something else...something more acceptable, more responsible, one with less risk and had a brighter final outcome.

Only after making the decision or a series of decisions like this, they find they are miserable because there has always been a mismatch with what they really wanted in their life and what they ended up choosing. So in finally choosing to live in a regret free zone, they are saying that they are changing their story and making a leap into living the life they always imagined for themselves.

Making a jump like this does not occur in one fell swoop, it takes time to understand first that it is even possible and then to decipher what that imagined life looks like. There are steps in the process that can free us from our own limited beliefs as well as dissolving the way we think about how the world will view our change.

So often we care more about what others think so we will stay stuck in place just so we don't rock the boat. Once we shed the concern about what others are thinking, we can then focus on what we think is best for ourselves. This is not to say that we don't look around and see how our actions can impact our family, but it is not done in a selfish manner but rather in an attempt to finally uncover what our essential self has been trying to tell us all these years!

How To Make The Shift?

One of the first steps in the process is to understand that a change is needed. It can be felt as a gut feeling or a general feeling that something is not quite right, doesn't fit and a change might need to occur. There are a variety of ways that we can become exposed to the need for change such as in conversations, paying attention to how we feel in our bodies, acknowledgment of the longing within or having a synchronistic encounter where suddenly we come face to face with what it is that we wish we could do.

There is a subtle shift that is occurring internally that we may not yet be aware of. This shift is an acknowledgement that change is afoot or that change may be coming our way. As time goes by this shift comes more to the surface and is no longer a hidden longing. We begin to glimpse the way forward. Usually at this stage we feel nervous and anxious and wonder how we will be able to achieve our goal. We are still mired in the present and aware of the circumstances that have us in this current situation.

Perhaps out of necessity and responsibility we understand why we are where we are and there is fear and anxiety about making changes in our lifestyle. Regret often surfaces when we finally get clear around the fact that we wanted to make a change but we stayed put, felt trapped and never made any attempt toward moving toward our heart's desire. We acknowledge that perhaps we didn't know how or to trust ourselves fully.

Many people are able to acknowledge and then create a vision for where they are headed while standing in the very place where they feel stuck and trapped. They also create action steps that will lead them toward living the life they always imagined. It may take years to create that life you want and it can be in process while moving about in your current situation.

The shift occurs in the belief that the vision can be accomplished "if" the plan is adhered to. We see so many people fail in their New Years Resolutions and other goals because they stop doing the very steps that will take them to the goal. Weight Watchers meetings caution to write down every bite so the client has the awareness and accountability needed to reach their desired weight loss goal.

What seems less clear is how to plan for the future you have always dreamed of, long before a retirement or a job layoff happens. We all know folks these days who are living lives of quiet desperation, wishing, hoping, fingers crossed, that another life could be lived. When they wish for another life, they immediately chastise themselves for wanting more than they have today. They chide themselves for thinking "maybe" and cast doubt on themselves that they aren't grateful enough for what they have been given.

It is okay to want more, to become aligned, finally with what your passion is in life. Many people believe staying stuck is their lot in life. It doesn't have to be when you have the ability to shift your belief system to a place where you can imagine your future as possible!

CREATIVE TRANSFORMATION

When we grasp onto the vision we have created for the future and have begun to take the action steps that will move us toward our goal, there are subtle changes that take begin to take place in our thinking. Even though we may still be anchored firmly in our present, we begin to daydream more and more about the future as seen in our vision and now it starts to become clearer as we spend time mentally tweaking it. The tweaking may alter the vision somewhat, maybe making it clearer by seeing it in vivid color or adding more to it to make it even more of what we long for.

There comes a point where we notice that our thinking has changed and we are more in alignment with this vision for our life and willing to take the steps needed in order to make it happen. There seems to be an urgency to get going and not to waste time. Some folks seem unable to envision or think that taking time to envision the big picture is a useless exercise. Some of these same folks are ones who are worried about change. They think it scary and judge it is safer to stay right where they are and so it is not surprising to discover that they are in the same place at a later date. Nothing has changed yet there is a longing for the things they did not do, the chances they never took. They believed that playing it safe was the best thing for them. Perhaps it was, but the end result was not what they wanted.

Creative transformation occurs because we open ourselves to change and we understand that there will be some tasks that be hard for us. We take this as a given when we get to those points, we nod in understudying because we expected some bumps in the road on our journey. The goal is to get from here to there...to cross the bridge from our present life to our future life and to make it real.

If we imagine that on the side of the road leading to this bridge there are stakes in the ground with signs indicating the various stages and changes that will happen before we cross the bridge and then on the other side of the road are a series of stakes in the ground between the milestone stakes on the right, listing the actions that must be undertaken before one can advance to the next milestone, then we can see clearly an overview of how it happens.

Making Your Future Real

Oprah often mentions about living your "right life." In our context we will use the concept of the right life as the future we wish we were living right now. Many people seem to believe that a fairy godmother or a lottery win are how we get to live that right life. They do not realize that their future is created by their own imagination and action steps and is in their own hands to craft. It is not something that will be handed to you.

Once envisioned, it begins right where you are. It is possible to continue living out your life just as you are but the change begins with the deep understanding that you want more, a different life than the one you are living now. Once that understanding comes and you are ready to imagine freely about what that right life/future can be, it becomes easier to make it happen.

Do you dream at night and upon wakening lose the dream as soon as you open your eyes? This is why it is crucial to write down the pieces of the future you imagine in as much detail as you can. It can then be changed to reflect our hearts desire.

Do-Overs, Second Chances and Second Journey's

Do-overs give us another opportunity to do it the way we want.

- What do-over would move me closer to my desired future?
- What lesson could I learn by performing a do-over?

Second chances give us the opportunity to explore "what if's"

- What if I had the money to do something else?
- What if I had the time to do something else?
- What would that be?

With each stage, we look to move forward into the zone where we have no regrets. We learn to care less about what others think and more about what our heart's desire may be.

Second and third journeys usually indicate a deliberate change made with understanding and knowledge of what this journey will look like and how it might end up. Sometimes this is called the second or third act in a person's life.

- What would my second journey look like
- Describe what would my third journey look like?
- What would take my breath away?

If my plan, for instance, is to travel the world in the lap of luxury but, I haven't saved enough for my basic needs, then I need to understand that I save and do without other items so that I can plan a particular trip. It may be in my car or on the bus instead of by a cruise ship but dreaming about the future also needs to take into consideration the reality of time, money and physical health.

Creating The Life You Only Imagined

This book has attempted to give you various ways to change your life from the one you are currently living to one that is more in alignment with who you are and with who you are becoming.

I'd like to end with a quote from a wall hanging in my office. It greets me each day and says,

---

Live your life with intention
Live the life you've always dreamed of,
The life you have always imagined living.

Go for it with gusto!

Lorrie

JOURNAL EXERCISES:

Exercise 58 – Can you see how you will get over the bridge to the goal?

Exercise 59 – Starting right where you are - write out how you will get from here to there.

Acknowledgments

I would like to thank those who have helped me along the journey I traveled to create my own future mead real.

For my husband of 47 years, Rob, for seeing long before I could the potential within me to be the woman that I am today.

For my daughter Sally, who patiently typed up the first draft of this book from a notebook full of penciled paragraphs and for my son Steve, who designed the book cover - thank you for the hundreds of small ways you support me.

For my writing pal, Av, who has challenged and encouraged me toward publishing a 6-year old draft and helped me to be brave and unafraid of the process..

For my writing groups who encouraged me at every meeting to push myself harder and search to find the words that express on paper what has always been my heart's desire.

Study Guide

This study guide has been prepared for book clubs as well as our virtual book club on Facebook. If you would like to join this virtual option, please email me at: lorrieborchertbooks@gmail.com.

Chapter 1:

Can you relate to the potential experience or have you met an older adult who spends a great deal of time reminiscing and is full of regret?

Chapter 2:

Did this chapter take you on a personal journey through the decision making you made that has taken you to where you are today?

Chapter 3:

What do you wish you had done differently? Are you able to own your role in how you arrived at where you are?

Chapter 4:

Were you able to identify a sleeping or dormant dream or a passion that was important to you earlier in life?

Chapter 5:

Were you encouraged to wake up that dream and make it or part of it into a reality in your life? How could you start?

Chapter 6:

Do you find yourself having to do things over? Frequently? What was there about the do-over chapter that seemed true and relevant to you?

Chapter 7:

If you were given the ticket for a second chance, share what you would do with it. What would change in your life? What action steps would you use to make the change?

Chapter 8:

What does your next chapter look like? Has this book helped to crystalize what that could be? Or at least given you a vague outline for what you could change to reach your future life?

Chapter 9:

Has the important of having a roadmap and action steps resonated with you? How can you use this tool in your own life?

Chapter 10:

How have the exercises at the end of each chapter or the journal companion helped you to map out and create your own future?

Do you want to live in a zone of no-regret? How will you get there?

The Story Behind the Story

The thread of no-regrets has surfaced again and again in my life. First with relatives that died and I had regretted not getting more of their life's story before they passed.

Then with 5 wonderful aging women who helped with my master's thesis. They all shared in various ways their experience with having regrets as they looked back over their lives. Although I was assessing cognitive function in aging, the topic of having no regrets seemed like something I wanted to know more about.

I have developed a series of books entitled: Living Big with No Regrets and will be working on subsequent books about bucket lists adventures to add to this series. Stay tuned!

About the Author

An avid reader, Lorrie has wanted to be a writer since the age of ten. As a 70th birthday present to herself, she finally succeeded in becoming a published author of substance with her first book.

She is both a writer and a certified Martha Beck Life Coach and lives in Vero Beach, Florida with her husband Rob and her ginger cat, Miep.

For more information contact me at:

www.futuresmadereal.com
lorrieborchertbooks@gmail.com

Also by Lorrie Borchert

A Journal Companion for A Practical Guide For Making Your Future Real

Made in the USA
Middletown, DE
09 February 2022

60876536R00057